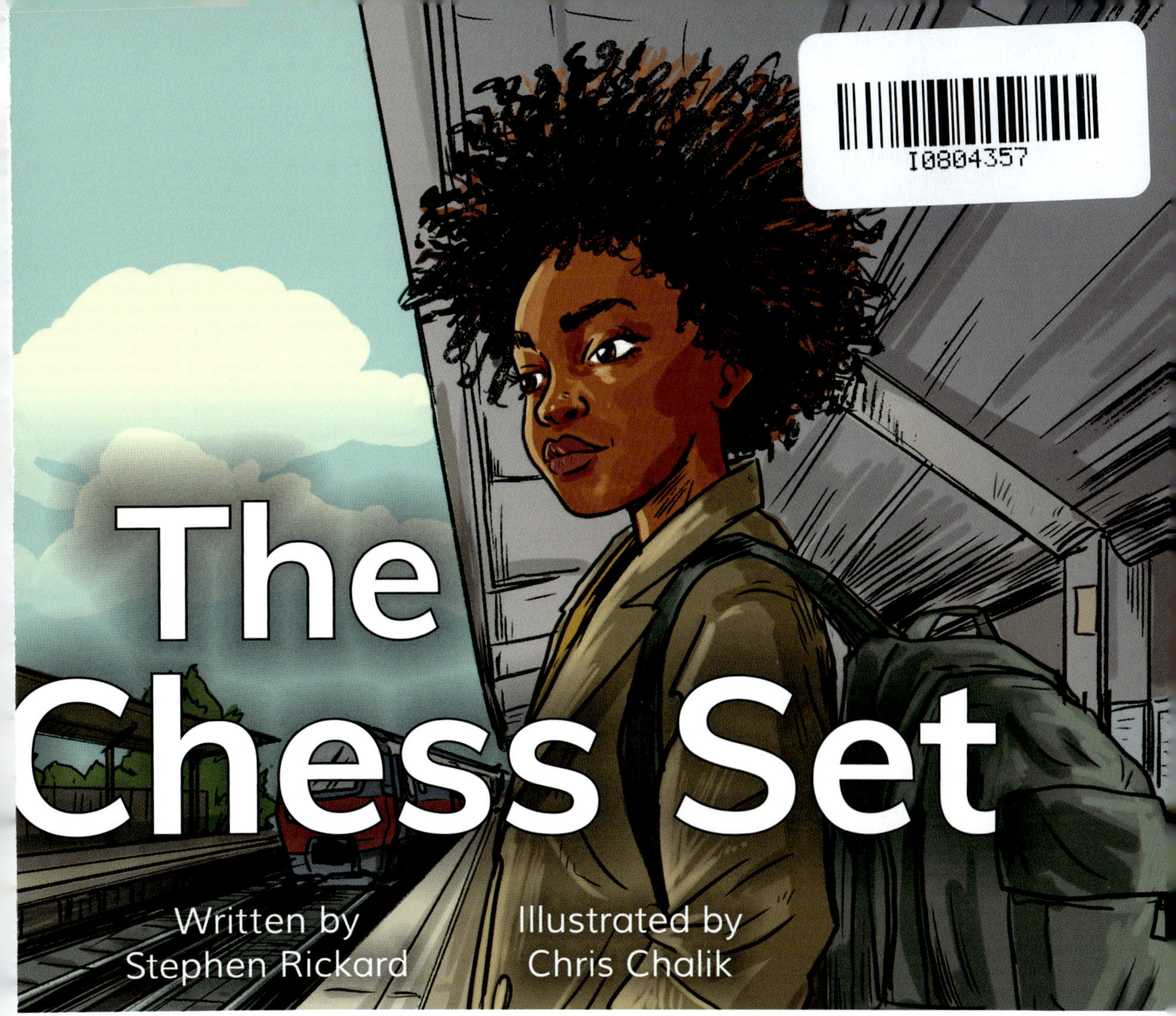

The Chess Set

Written by
Stephen Rickard

Illustrated by
Chris Chalik

Published in 2026 by
Norwood House Press
2544 Clinton Street
Buffalo, NY 14224

Printed in the United States of America

Library of Congress Cataloging-in-Publication Data:
Names: Rickard, Stephen, 1957-, author. | Hawkins, Daisy, author. | Atkins, Jill (Children's author). | Chalik, Chris, illustrator.
Title: The chess set / written by Stephen Rickard, illustrated by Chris Chalik. Mushroom power / written by Daisy Hawkins. Bonkers beach huts / written by Jill Atkins.
Description: Buffalo, NY : Norwood House Press, 2026. | Series: Phonics all-stars: phase 5a
Identifiers: ISBN 9781978578951 (pbk.) | ISBN 9781978578968 (library bound) | ISBN 9781978578975 (ebook)
Subjects: LCSH: Reading–Phonetic method–Juvenile fiction. | English language–Phonetics–Juvenile fiction. | Time travel–Juvenile fiction. | Mushrooms–Juvenile fiction. | Beaches–Juvenile fiction.
Classification: LCC LB1573.3 R534 2026 | DDC 372.465–dc23

CPSIA compliance information: Batch #CW26NHP: For further information contact Norwood House Press at 1-800-237-9932.

Tabitha Green was a big chess fan. She had a little pocket chess set, and she cherished it so much that she'd even carved the letters TG on the back.

Tabitha lived with her dad. Her mom had died when Tabitha was little.

Today, Tabitha was going shopping in Tatford. She slipped the chess set into her pocket. She liked to play chess on the train.

On the train, Tabitha fell asleep. When the train stopped at Tatford, it made her wake up with a start.

In a panic, she grabbed her bag and jumped off.

Tabitha looked up and down the platform. There were no people to be seen – not even a porter or ticket collector.

Then she looked at the list of trains leaving Tatford. It had a date of 1993. How odd!

Tabitha left the platform and had a big shock. The roads, shops, cars, and people of Tatford were no longer there. It was just trees and a mud track.

Then Tabitha saw a girl playing in a tree.

"Come and play with me," said the girl. "It's fun high up in the trees."

Tabitha and the girl spent the rest of the day playing. They had a fantastic day.

At the end of the day, Tabitha got a battered, moth-eaten train back to her dad's.

When Tabitha got back, the chess set was not in her pocket. It must have dropped out when she was up in the trees, in Tatford.

Tabitha was upset.

"Mom gave you that chess set when you were little," said Dad. "It's such a shame that it got lost."

The next day, Dad came into Tabitha's room with a box.

"I've just found this in the loft," he said. "I've never seen it until now. It has 'TG' on it."

Tabitha lifted the lid. She was looking at a pocket chess set, just like the one she had lost.

Tabitha looked on the back. She saw the letters TG carved on the case.

Was this her chess set?

If it was, how did it get in the loft?

Did it have something to do with the girl she had met in Tatford?

In 1993, Mom had been about thirteen too.
That girl Tabitha had met in Tatford ... Had it been her mom?

Mushroom Power
By Daisy Hawkins

People all around the globe like to eat mushrooms.

You might have tried chestnut mushrooms, white button mushrooms, or oyster mushrooms.

Nevertheless, mushrooms can do so much for us. They are not just our dinner.

You might think that all mushrooms are white or light brown, but this is not true.

In fact, mushrooms come in all sorts of exotic reds, greens, and blues.

Mushrooms can get quite big too.

Some mushrooms light up at night.

We think that they might be attracting insects with their greenish light.

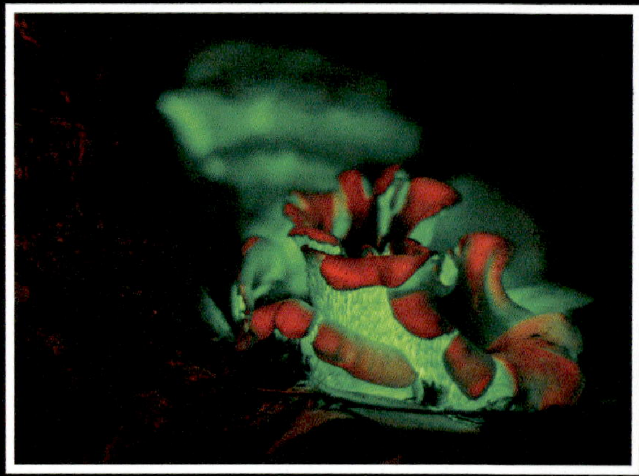

Or maybe the mushrooms are just saying, "I look odd, so do not eat me!"

Some animals like to eat mushrooms, just as we do.

Birds, slugs, and, yes, squirrels will eat mushrooms.

Meanwhile, some mushrooms eat animals!

They can spear, trap, and kill little organisms for food.

There are some mushrooms too that can attack ants and feed on them. That's the sort of thing you might see in a horror film!

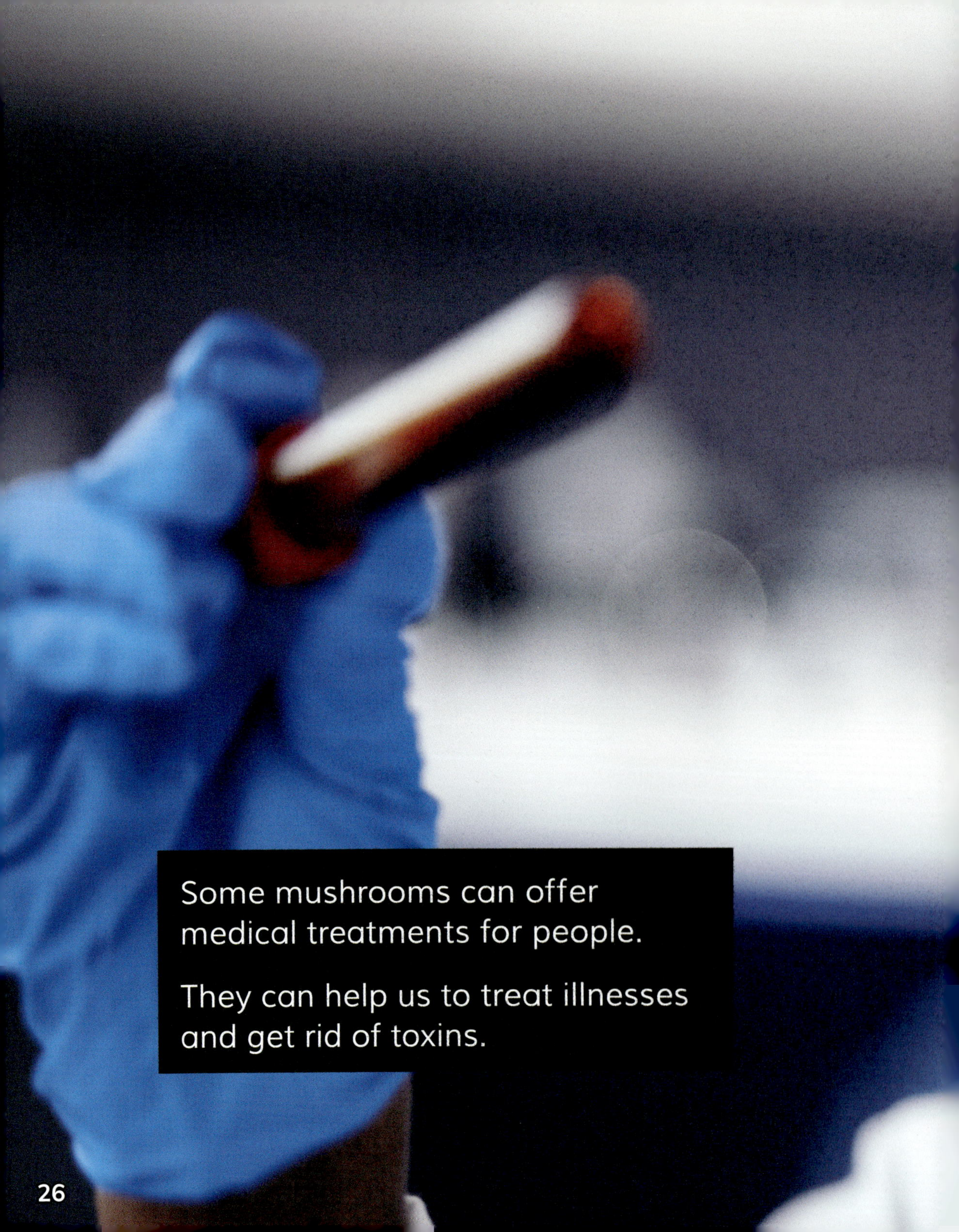

Some mushrooms can offer medical treatments for people.

They can help us to treat illnesses and get rid of toxins.

We think that some sorts of mushrooms allow trees to chat.

The mushrooms connect the trees together, and can tell each tree if there is a lack of rain, or if there are attacks from insects.

Some people say this phenomenon is "the wood-wide web."

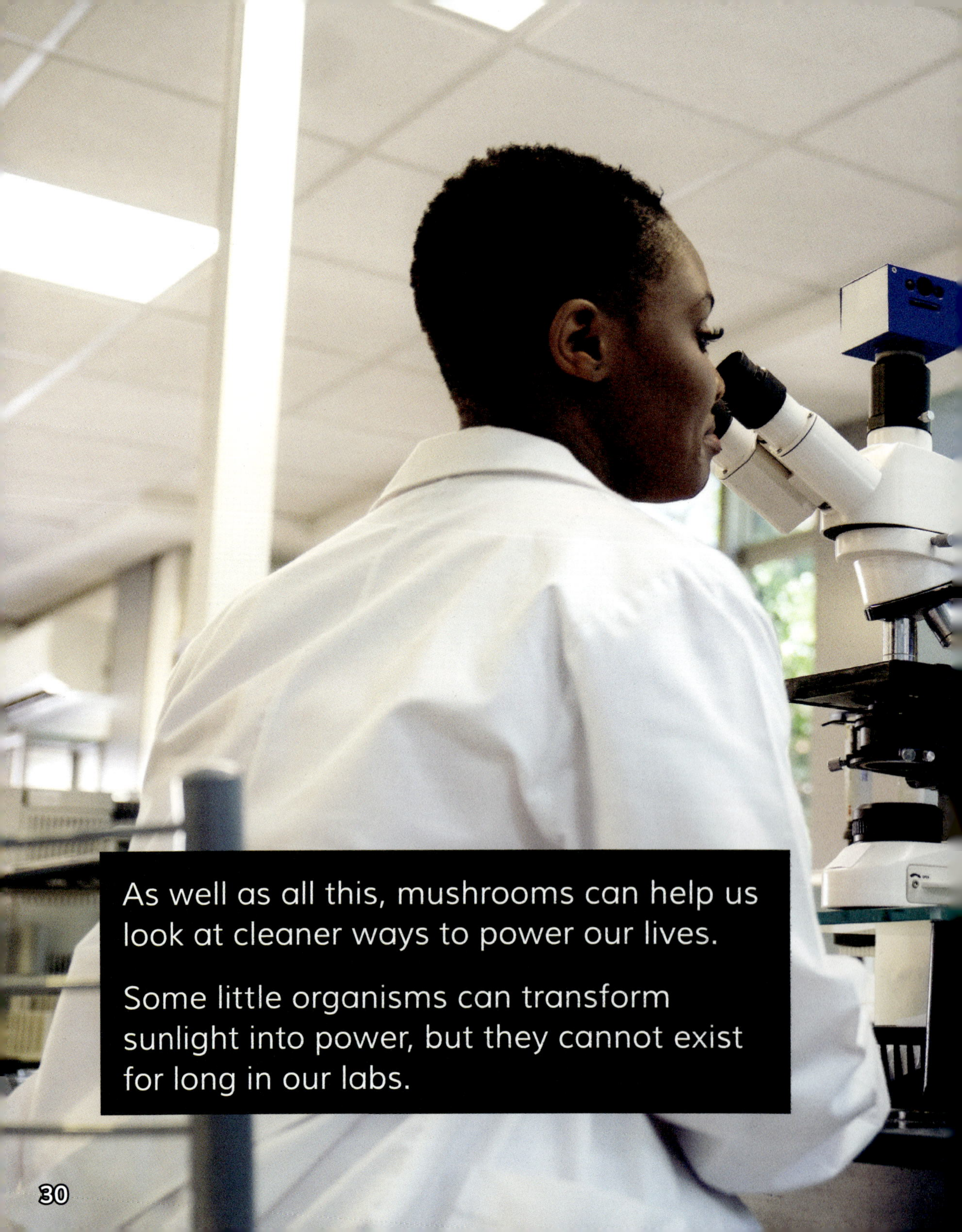

As well as all this, mushrooms can help us look at cleaner ways to power our lives.

Some little organisms can transform sunlight into power, but they cannot exist for long in our labs.

However, if the organisms are kept on mushrooms, they can exist for longer.

That way, there is time for us to look into whether the organisms can help us in our hunt for green power, without needing oil or gas.

All hail the might of the modest little mushroom!

Bonkers Beach Huts

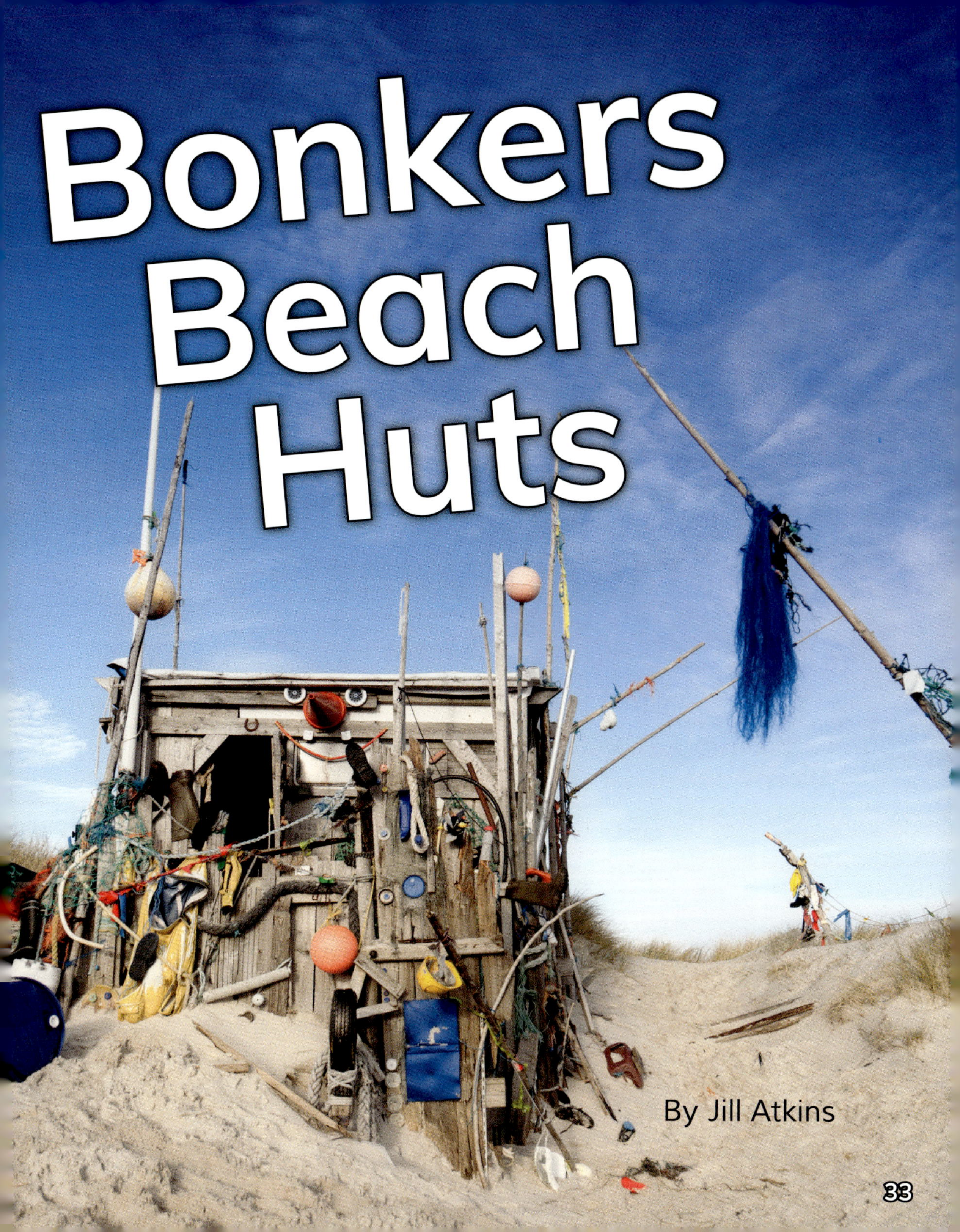

By Jill Atkins

Have you ever seen beach huts at the coast?

Beach huts are little box homes, often made of wood. You can see them next to the beach, all in a line and all looking the same – just like these blue and white striped huts.

Sometimes, the beach huts are so bright.

Is it a bit extreme? You might need to squint when you look at them!

This is an entire town of beach huts.

If you go to the beach "to get away from it all," this is not the best beach to visit!

These beach huts have an upstairs and a downstairs. I think that's bonkers!

The inside of a beach hut is so important. You need to decorate it well. It needs to be a home away from home.

You will need chairs, boxes to keep things in, a line to hang up wet towels – and a way to make a drink.

If it rains at the beach, you may spend a lot of time inside.

You can look out at the people getting wet.

In distant lands, you might see some exotic beach huts.

This hut is a look-out, in case people need to be rescued from the sea.

Way back, when even cars had not been invented, rich people sometimes had a beach hut like this.

It was a wagon on wheels and it was taken down to the sea with someone inside.

When it reached the sea, you just slipped out for a swim.

You can have a beach hut on the beach, near the sea.

Or you can go one step further, and have a beach hut in the sea.

These huts are people's homes.

This one is floating!

Are you rich? Then these beach huts might be just right for you.

If you are not rich, you might as well keep on dreaming.

You can make a beach hut from the things that have been left on the beach.

It might look bonkers, but it will stand out from the crowd!